CRAZY STRING GAMES

INCLUDING CATS CRADLE

Published 2000 by

Hinkler Books Pty Ltd

17-23 Redwood Drive

Dingley, Victoria, 3172, Australia

© Hinkler Books Pty Ltd, 2000

First Printed 2000

Written by: Barb Whiter

ISBN: 1 86515 265X

Printed and bound in China.

CONTENTS

ALL ABOUT STRING GAMES

With just one loop of string and your ten fingers (and, occasionally, with the help of your teeth or feet!) you can make wonderful magic shapes. These shapes could be a bed, a witch's broom, diamonds, butterflies, and ladders.

There are a couple of easy 'base' moves to learn which, as the name suggests, are the base for many of the shapes, so if you learn these well, you're well on the way to having lots of fun.

String games can be played by one, which is perfect because you start and stop the game when you've had enough or your hands and fingers are getting tired. This could happen if you practise and play a bit too long.

Other games, such as the world-renowned Cat's Cradle can begin with one person, but to get the most enjoyment from it, the game needs two people who are pretty much of an equal standard in their experience of string games. So grab this book and the cord as well as your best friend and learn together!

They are some of the world's most universal games. This means that an Arctic Inuit child, a Navajo child, an Australian Aboriginal child and a child from any of the African, European or Asian countries, especially Japan, as well as a child on a beach in the South Pacific would all know some form of string games.

And because the cultures are different, the types of 'string' used are very different too. Nowadays we in developed countries would use nylon cord or white string; elastic is also used. However, if you were a child from a South Pacific island beach you may use left-over fishing line, or thin rope created from fibre from a tree or vine. Inuit children may use sinew or a thin leather strip known as a thong. A strong twine can be made from bark... and some cultures even use braided human hair... and so it goes on.

ALL ABOUT STRING GAMES...
AND HOW TO MAKE YOUR OWN STRING

Of course you will have realised that this wonderful book already comes with its own cord, so everything is ready for you to go straight into learning all the fun games within its pages.

But, accidents happen. What if you lose your cord, or your best friend takes it home one night by mistake and you really, really want to practise, or you actually leave it at someone's house one day?

Don't worry, another piece of cord can be used. Or you can give your best friend a present of her own cord, so she doesn't mistakenly borrow yours!

You need anywhere from 70 cm (27½ inches) to one metre (39 inches) of your chosen cord and it's best to join the ends with one of those little metal joiners you can find in haberdashery stores which grab each end and then you flatten them together very hard (although these can come apart at crucial moments!).

Or you can melt the ends of the cord together. You can only melt the cord if it is nylon or another synthetic. It's best to do this with an adult.

1.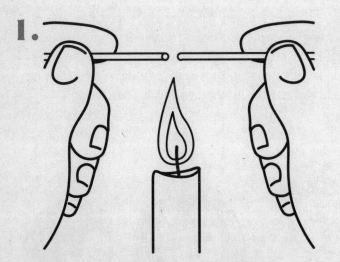

Hold both ends of the string near each other about two centimetres (nearly an inch) above a candle flame. Be careful, but if the ends are not melting at all, they are too far away, bring them closer. If the ends begin burning or singeing you are too close!

2.

When the ends are gooey, hold them together (without touching the hot bits!).

3.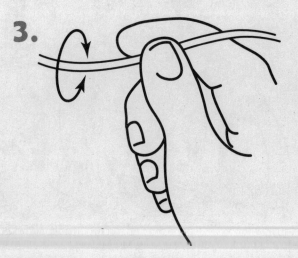

Count to five or maybe ten to make sure they are cool, and then roll the ends between your fingers to smooth the join.

The third best choice is to knot it with a knot that won't slip, such as a reef knot. Follow the diagrams to create the perfect knot:

1.

Lay the right end over the left.

4.

Put this new left end under the new right end and tighten by pulling on all four ends to close the knot up.

2.

Put this right end under the left to begin the knot.

5.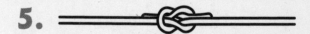

Trim the ends as close as possible to make the knot neat and so it will have less interference in the sliding and moving of the cord during the games.

3.

Lay what is now the new left end across the new right end.

TERMS USED IN STRING GAMES

Study the pair of hands below and become familiar with the terms used for each finger and for each string with regard to where it is looped.

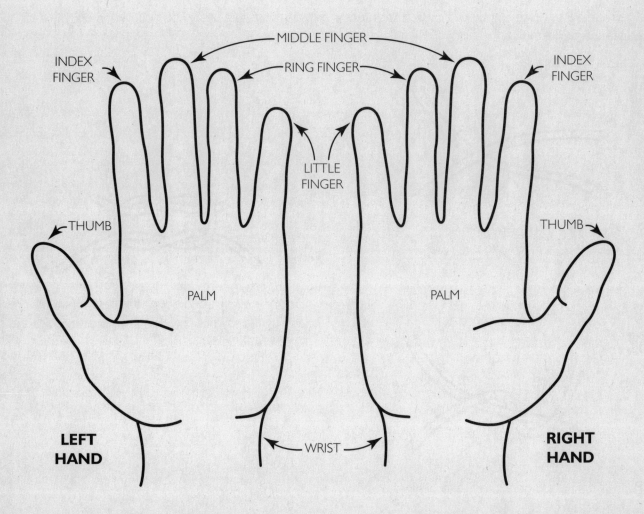

So, when a string goes around a finger or thumb, it makes a loop. These loops then take their names from their location on your hands - thumb loop, index loop, middle finger loop, ring finger loop and little finger (or pinkie!) loop.

If you move an index loop to a thumb, it becomes a thumb loop and so on.

Each loop has a near string - the one closer to you - and a far string - yes, that's right - the one further away from you.

If there are two loops on your thumb or finger, one is called the lower loop - that's the one near the base or bottom of your finger or thumb - and the upper loop - obviously the one near the top of your thumb or finger.

As you make the figures and shapes in this book you will use your fingers and thumbs to weave the strings in set patterns. Sometimes you'll be asked to drop or release a loop from your fingers - this can be difficult but after practise it becomes easier.

INDEX FINGER AND MIDDLE FINGER BASES

Begin by teaching yourself these two base beginnings. Many tricks start in either of these ways. They are known as the index finger base and the middle finger base. We'll begin with the index finger base:

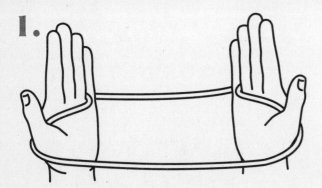

1.

Start by looping the string across both palms and behind your little fingers and thumbs.

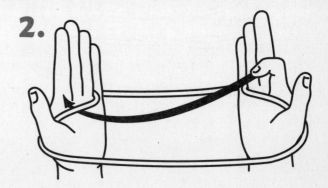

2.

Now using the index finger of your right hand, pick up the string running across the left palm.

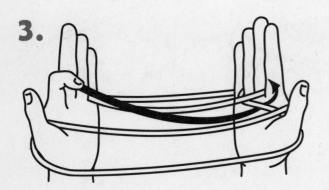

3.

Pull your hands apart.

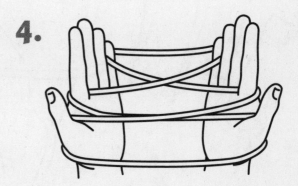

4.

Complete the move by reaching your index finger of your left hand across to pick up the string running across the right palm, and pull your hands apart. That's the index finger base movement completed.

I.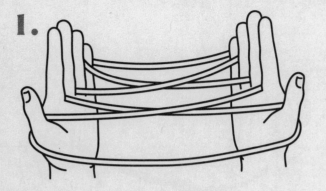

Begin at the starting position and using your middle fingers of both hands, repeat steps 2, 3 and 4 to complete the middle finger base movement.

A TIP: always make your index and middle finger bases by first picking up the string from the palm of your left hand.

Sometimes you'll be instructed to share a loop between two fingers, or a finger and a thumb. This is how it's done - without dropping all the other loops or strings.

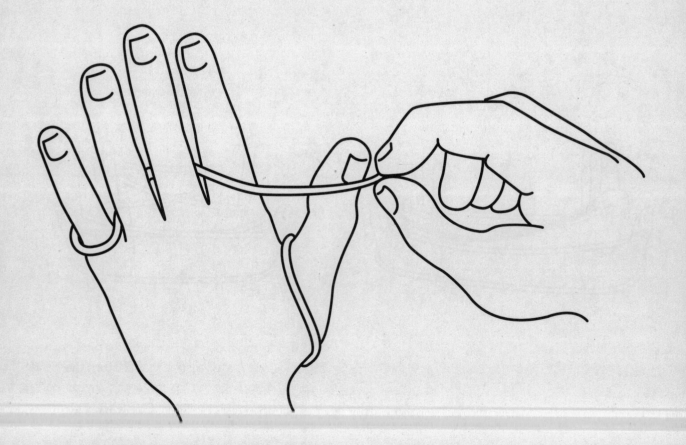

Simply use your opposite index finger if it is free to pull out the loop so that the other finger or thumb will be able to fit into the loop too.

START SIMPLY

CUP AND SAUCER

If you've practised doing the index and middle finger bases you'll be nearly there with this simple, effective, first effort!

1.

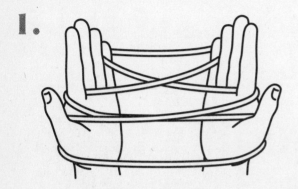
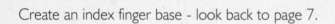

Create an index finger base - look back to page 7.

2.

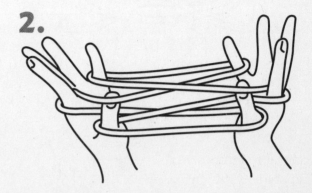

Now using both thumbs at once, reach across to the far index string (the diagram above will help, as will the diagram on terms used on page 6), hooking the string.

3.

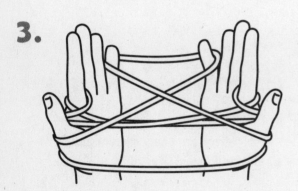

Pull your thumbs back to where they began complete with the extra string. You now have two loops on each thumb.

4.

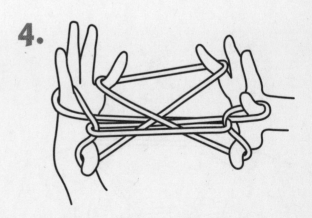

Either by clever wiggling, or with the help of your mouth, pull the bottom loops off your thumbs, taking them over the top loops. Keep checking the diagrams (above) - they'll help!

5.

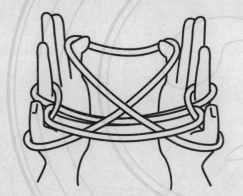

Now you need to drop the loops from both of your little fingers... carefully!

And pull your hands apart. Can you see anything resembling a cup and saucer?

6.

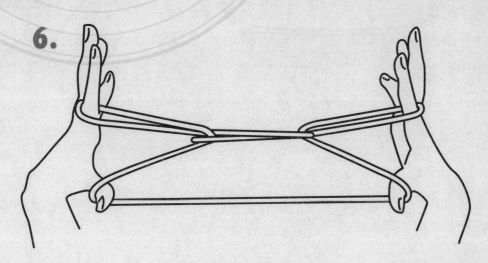

That's right - tilt your thumbs upwards and now the cup and saucer are easily recognised! Well done, that's your first successful shape! Easy isn't it!

7.

EIFFEL TOWER

This is also very easy. If you've managed to do the Cup and Saucer - you can do this in seconds! In fact, just follow the instructions previously given for the Cup and Saucer and keep it on your fingers. And now read on.

Next, just grab the string which makes the top of the cup in your teeth...

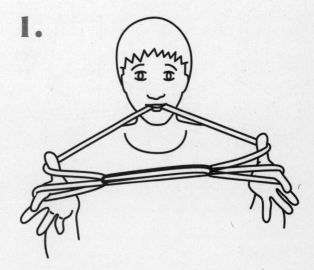

1.

... then drop both loops from your thumbs, and pull your hands down very gently - keeping the string tight in your teeth. But don't pull the strings too tight, or it just won't work! If you are doing this alone, you'll need a mirror to enjoy your talent!

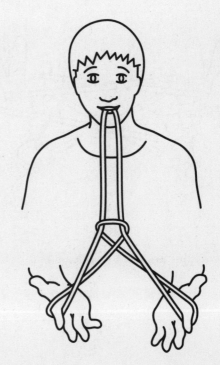

2.

THUMB TRAP

Another pretty easy string game (from Japan) which is great for boosting your repertoire - time for a show around the dinner table at home now!

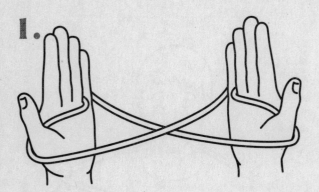

Start by looping the cord around your little fingers and thumbs as if you were beginning normally. However, this time just give the loop one twist - see diagram.

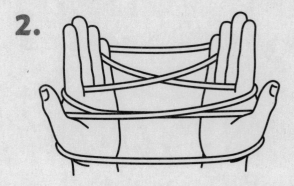

Now make the index finger base (see page 7).

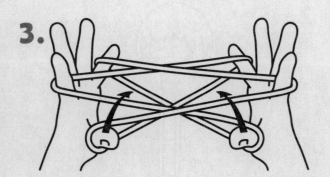

Place your thumbs into the index finger loop as shown above.

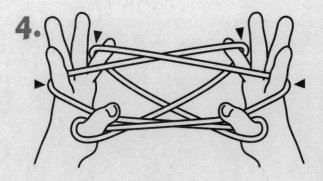

Carefully hold the strings underneath your thumbs, while releasing both loops from your left and right index fingers and little fingers.

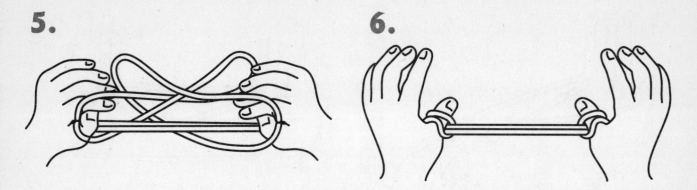

5.

You can easily release these strings by bending both hands inwards - the strings will slide off.

6.

Now pull your hands apart and both thumbs will be trapped inside a loop of string!

WITCH'S BROOM

This string game is also called Fish Spear (from northern Queensland in Australia) or Crow's Feet (from American Native Indian tribal history). It's a quick, impressive show for the family!

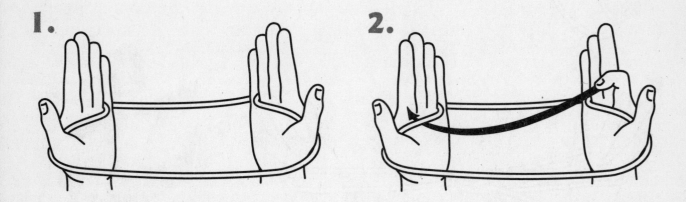

1.

Begin as usual with the cord being looped around your little fingers and thumbs (see diagram).

2.

Use your index finger from your right hand and hook it under the string that runs across your left palm, but don't pull your hands apart yet.

3.

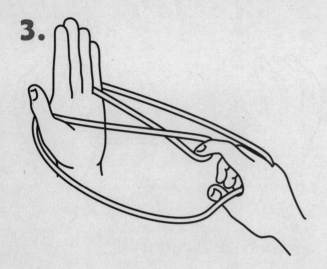

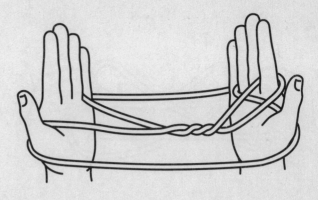

Twist this new loop by twirling your index finger around it twice... and then pull your hands apart.

4.

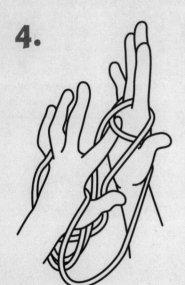

The next step is to reach across with your left index finger and hook the string running across your right palm. Just reach through the loop you've twisted to pick up the string.

5.

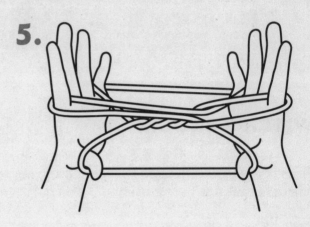

Pull your hands apart now.

6.

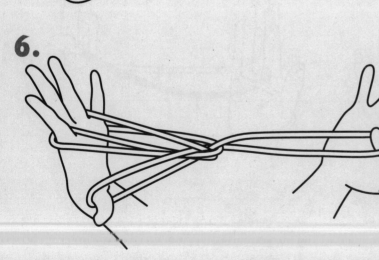

Finally, drop the loops from both the thumb and little finger of your right hand and pull your hands apart until the strings are tight. Here's your Witch's Broom - or Fish Spear - or Crow's Feet.

RABBIT IN A HAT

Another easy one person shape game.

1.

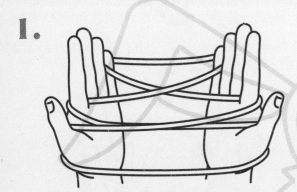

Begin by creating an index finger base and open your hands out.

2.

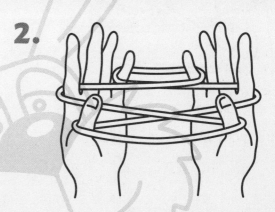

Both your thumbs are to be taken over the thumb near and far strings and hooked under and up through the middle of the index string. The string will be resting on the back of your thumbs.

3.

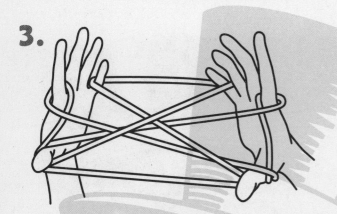

Bring the strings forward so you now have two loops around your thumbs

4.

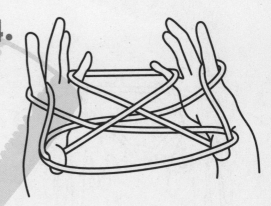

Now things get a bit tricky! You need to take the big bottom loop over the top of the smaller loop on each thumb and slip them off your thumbs completely. This leaves you with the top loop being the only loop left on your thumb.

5.

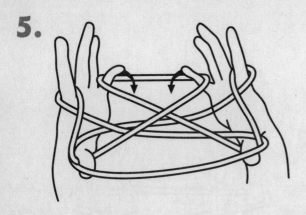

Drop the loops off both little fingers.

6.

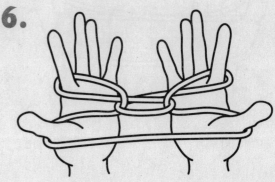

Now stretch out your hands, keeping the thumbs right out, and you should be able to see a rabbit's head, complete with wiggling ears.

7.

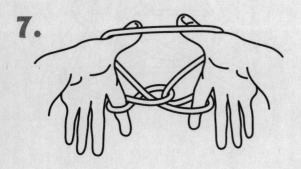

If you want to see the rabbit in the hat, you actually need to turn your hands over so your thumbs are up in the air and - hey presto! The rabbit turns into a top hat!

BUTTERFLY

A final easy one person string game which continues on from the rabbit on the previous page.

1.

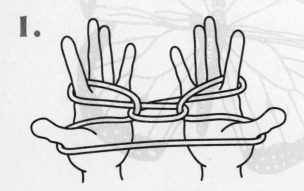

Begin by creating the rabbit on page 16.

2.

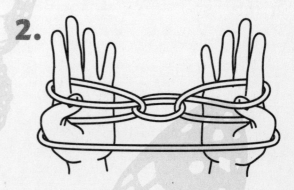

Push both thumbs up and over the index finger loops and lift them over your thumbs.

3.

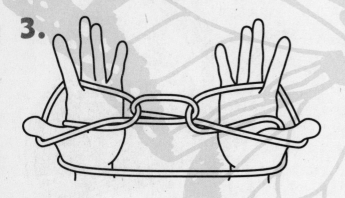

As done in the rabbit, now lift the bottom loops from your thumbs over the top loops and release them from your thumbs. If wiggling your thumbs doesn't work use your teeth!

4.

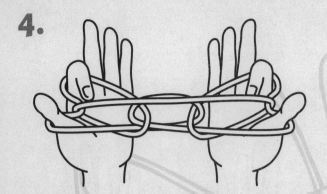

Next step is to hook both index fingers over the long, straight string across the middle of the display and down into the holes in front of your index fingers.

5.

Again, another tricky move. Grip the new index strings tightly, at the same time, tipping your hands over so the palms are both face down. Let the original index loops slide off your fingers.

6.

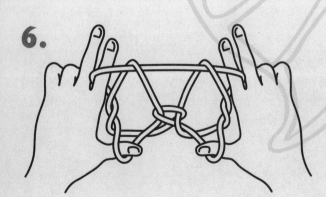

Now stretch out your hands and view your butterfly wanting to fly away!

READY FOR CAT'S CRADLE?

Cat's Cradle is one of the oldest of the string games. It probably travelled from Asia to Europe with the tea trade in the seventeenth century. And we know English children played the game around the 1780s when author, Charles Lamb, was writing about 'weaving cat's cradles' when he was at school.

The idea of the game is for two players (called first and second here) to continuously create and recreate the same order of figures or shapes by using the strings straight and also crossing them in X patterns. So one person holds the figure while the other picks up the Xs and takes them over, under or between the straight strings.

The players take turns to do both but you must make sure you are holding your strings securely before your partner removes their hands from the figure - otherwise, disaster!

Let's begin!

CAT'S CRADLE

(made by the first player)

1.

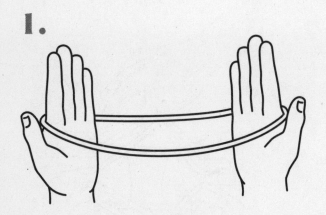

It's not the usual beginning because you place the string behind your hands - your thumbs aren't involved at this stage.

2.

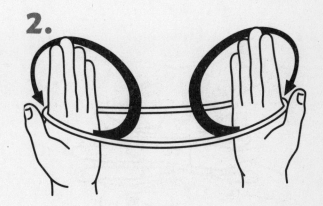

Take your right hand and loop the string around your left hand once more. Do the same with your left hand - loop it around your right hand once more. You now have the string looped across the back of your hands twice and across your palm just the once. The diagram above will help.

3.

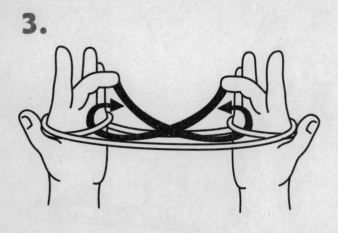

Now reach across with the middle finger of your right hand and hook the string running across your left palm. Pull your hands apart.

4.

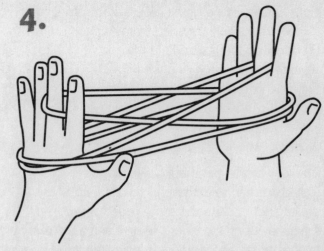

Repeat this action with the middle finger of your left hand - hooking the string crossing your right palm. And pull your hands apart. Now you've made Cat's Cradle.

CAT'S CRADLE... TO THE SOLDIER'S BED

(made by the second player)

Keep the Cat's Cradle on your hands and now your partner has a turn.

1.

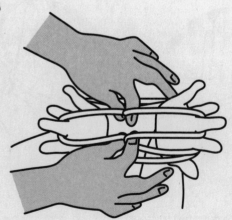

The second player looks straight down on the string and sees there are two Xs. Pinch them together, using your thumbs and index fingers, where they cross. (Check diagram above so you know you're right.)

2.

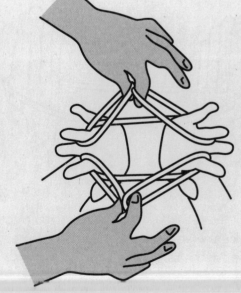

Keeping a hold of the Xs the second player pulls them out past the side strings - see diagram above.

3.

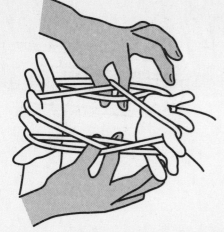

Now turn your hands over (still holding those Xs!), while at the same time taking your fingers down outside the strings, and then up into the wide, open centre.

4.

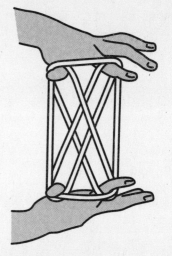

It's your turn to pull your hands apart, while your partner (first player) drops the strings, leaving you with The Soldier's Bed!

THE SOLDIER'S BED... TO CANDLES

(made by the first player)

Keep The Soldier's Bed on your hands and now your partner has a turn.

1.

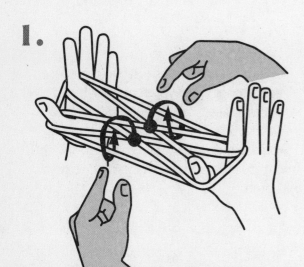

The first player is now going to do something very similar to what the second player just did - so we hope you were paying attention! Look for the two Xs and pinch them just where they cross. (It's easiest to find if you look down on the game.)

2.

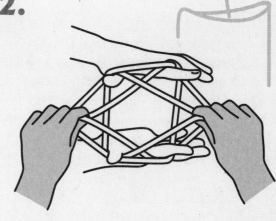

Keeping a tight grip on those Xs, you pull them out over the outside strings and then push your fingers under those same strings and up into the open centre of the game.

Pull your hands apart at the same time as your friend drops the strings from their hands. Now you've made Candles.

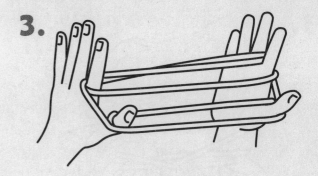

CANDLES TO THE MANGER

(made by the second player)

Keep Candles on your hands and now your partner has a turn.

1.

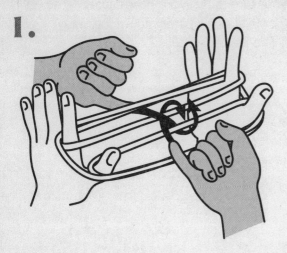

2.

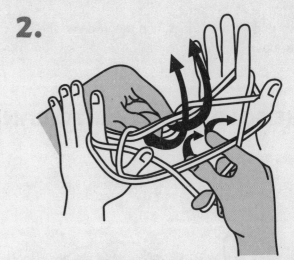

No more pinching Xs - this is a bit different. Using both little fingers, face up like a hook, you pull the right inside thumb string with your left little finger out over the outside string and hold it, and the left inside index string with your right little finger and hold that too. You should have made two triangles if you look down on them.

You need to keep a good strong hold of these little finger strings while you turn your hands over so your palms are face down. Now place both thumb and index finger of each hand together and push them down into the triangles, and then up and under the outside strings into the centre of the game.

3.

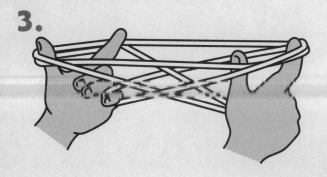

Still need to keep a tight hold of the little finger strings, while you pull your thumbs and index fingers apart. At this time your friend drops the strings from their hand and leaves you holding The Manger.

THE MANGER... TO DIAMONDS

(made by the first player)

Keep The Manger on your hands and now your partner has a turn.

1.

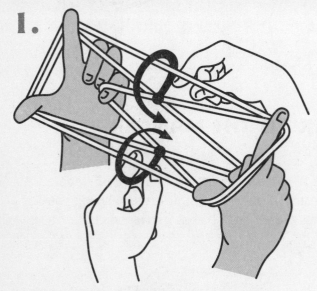

Look down on the strings and, using your index fingers and thumbs, take the two Xs from the outside and pull these strings out and up over the straight outside strings.

2.

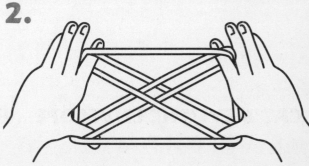

Keeping a tight grip, turn your hands over and push your pinching fingers into the open centre Now spread your fingers and pull your hands apart at the same time your friend lets go of the strings. So you can sparkle with Diamonds!

DIAMONDS... TO CAT'S EYE OR THE ENVELOPE

(made by the second player)

Keep Diamonds on your hands and now it's your partner's turn again.

Now these moves should feel familiar - yes, you've done them before to create The Soldier's Bed. So, here we go. Pinch the two Xs you can see. Lift them up and out over the outside strings.

1.

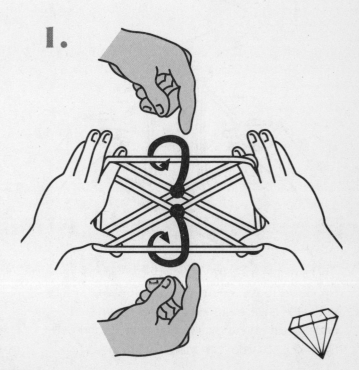

Then, still pinching hard, turn your index fingers and thumbs up into the centre of the game, and spread your fingers and hands apart at the same time your partner drops the strings. Now you've created The Cat's Eye or, if you prefer, The Envelope - yes, it does look like an envelope!

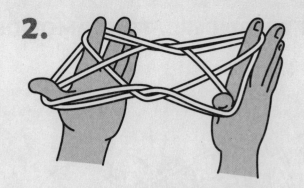

2.

CAT'S EYE/THE ENVELOPE... BACK TO THE MANGER

(to be made by the first player)

Keep Cat's Eye on your hands and let your partner have a go at something you created the first time around - but you started from a different set of strings. With the Cat's Cradle game this is how it goes - around and around. But wait, there are some extra difficult Cat's Cradle shapes to make soon.

1.

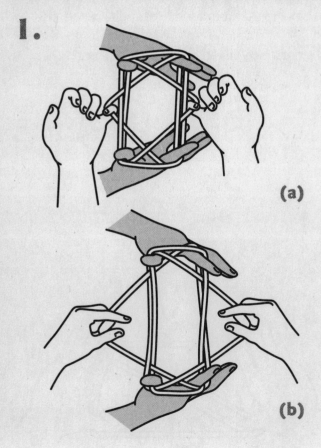

(a)

(b)

This is a little trickier! Look very carefully for the two short loops around the outside strings. Hook your little fingers into each of these from underneath (a)... look at the diagram!... and pull them out so wide they make two triangles (b).

2.

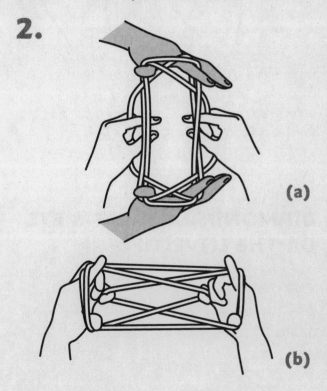

(a)

(b)

Put extra strength into your little fingers for this one and keep a good hold of the strings they are holding. Turn your hands over and push the thumb and index finger of each hand into the triangles under the outside strings and into the centre (a). Now pull your hands apart and spread your fingers while your friend drops their strings (b) - you're back to The Manger.

WHAT'S AFTER THE CAT'S CRADLE?

More Cat's Cradle - called Fish in a Dish actually! Of course, when people invent games, such as Cat's Cradle, there is always someone, somewhere who wants to do something different! We guess that person said, 'Let's not go back to The Manger, we'll try something new!' And these following games are what they discovered!

Instead of leaving The Cat's Eye/The Envelope move and returning to The Manger to create a round of Cat's Cradle, by keeping The Cat's Eye/The Envelope on your hands you can continue with the game by creating Fish in a Dish - miow!

FISH IN A DISH... FROM THE CAT'S EYE/THE ENVELOPE
...on page 23. This is made by the first player.

1.

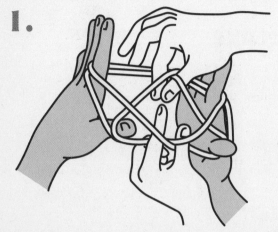

2.

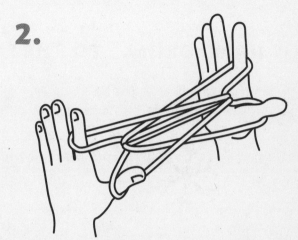

With your partner holding The Cat's Eye pattern, you use your index fingers and thumbs to hook on to the Xs at the sides of the central diamond where they meet the outside strings.

Now it's a simple move to push your thumb and index fingers up through the middle, and then pull out the pattern by stretching out your thumbs and index fingers and pulling apart your hands. At the same time your partner drops their strings.

There are two more shapes to make before finishing Cat's Cradle, so continue for The Hand Drum and The Snowflake.

THE HAND DRUM... FROM FISH IN A DISH
(made by the second player)

1.

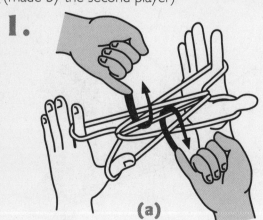

(a)

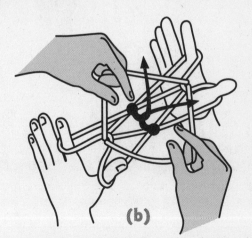

(b)

Can you see the straight strings in the centre of the pattern? Using both little fingers you need to hook these strings up and outside the pattern (a). Now you'll see two middle Xs that you want to grab (b) - at the same time as holding the strings with your little fingers - don't let go!

2.

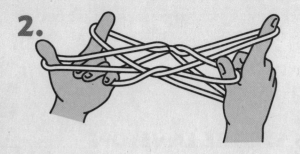

Now, not letting go of those little finger strings, you turn your index fingers and thumbs up through the central diamond shape (a) and pull the pattern out to its full extent (b) showing a little Hand Drum to play on. Of course your partner released their strings at the same time.

THE HAND DRUM... TO THE SNOWFLAKE

Finally, it's The Hand Drum... to The Snowflake (made by the first player)
Actually, you need another friend to complete the snowflake - three people and six hands!

There's only one step for this finale. Each person ends up with two loops of the Hand Drum pattern, so leave the second player happy for the moment with both index fingers occupied.

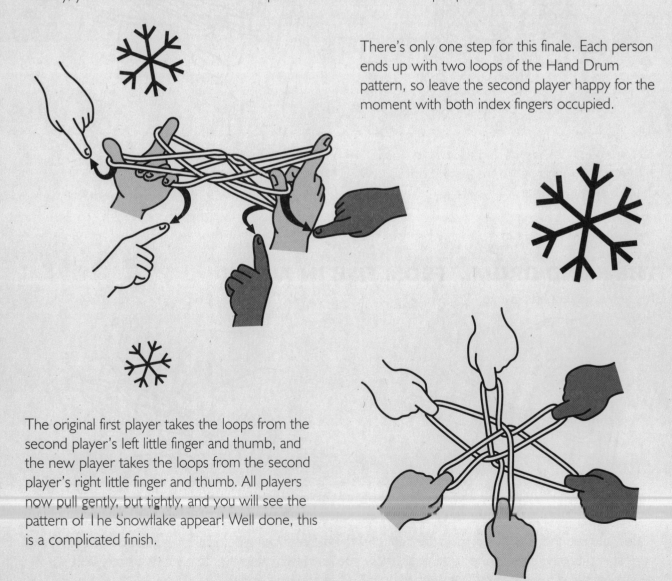

The original first player takes the loops from the second player's left little finger and thumb, and the new player takes the loops from the second player's right little finger and thumb. All players now pull gently, but tightly, and you will see the pattern of The Snowflake appear! Well done, this is a complicated finish.

SOME MORE COMPLICATED GAMES FOR ONE

If you are now back again playing with your own piece of cord on your own, but feel like trying something a little more complicated than the first easy patterns, after the challenges of Cat's Cradle, then these last three games are definitely for you.

JACOB'S LADDER

1.

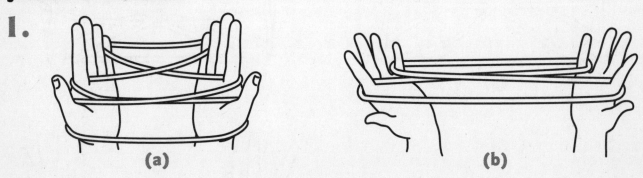

(a)   (b)

Begin this pattern by creating an index finger base (see page 7) (a) and then drop the loops from your thumbs (b).

2.

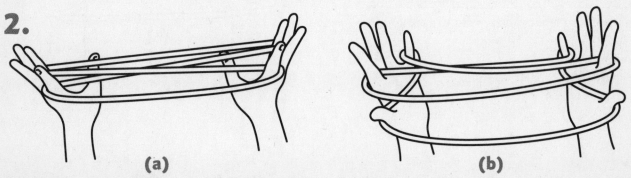

(a)   (b)

Reach under all the strings with your thumbs (keep an eye on the diagrams - they're there to help!) and hook the outside string with your thumbs from the outside (a). Pull this string back under all the others and spread your fingers apart (b).

3.

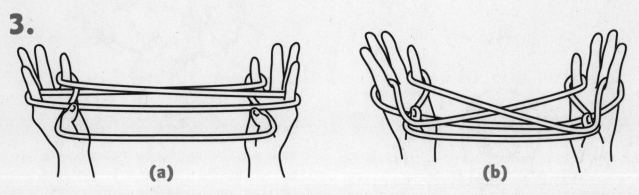

(a)   (b)

Be careful there's a tricky bit coming up! Your thumbs are needed to pick up another loop, but you must keep the loop already on your thumbs secure. Stretch both thumbs under the second string and hook them under the third string (a). Then pull this string back - hey presto! - two loops on each thumb (b).

4.

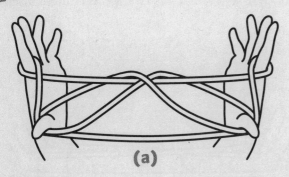

(a)

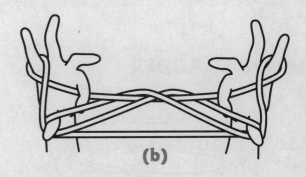

(b)

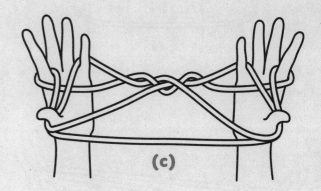

(c)

Drop the loops from both little fingers (a). Now use these freed-up little fingers to reach them over the string closest to them and hook under the next string (b). Pull the little fingers back to their normal position along with the string (c).

5.

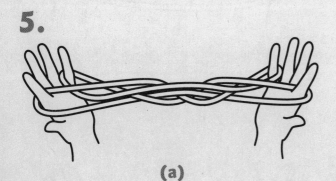

(a)

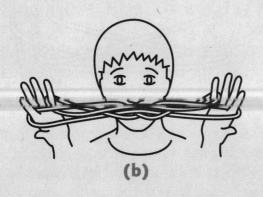

(b)

Free up your thumbs now by dropping all the loops from them ('a'). Stretch your fingers and hands apart and hold this string pattern up to your face - Cat's Whiskers! (b).

6.

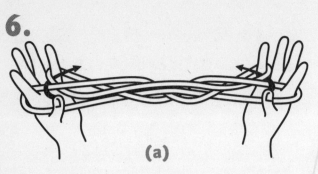 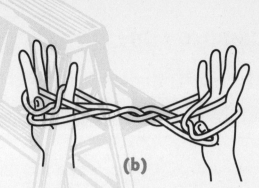

(a)   (b)

Although these whiskers looks very cute on you, we've nearly created Jacob's Ladder, so let's keep on going! Reach your thumbs across two strings and then hook them up under the third string away from you. Pull these strings back towards you (a). Now you need to pull the bottom section of the index finger loop on both hands back over the nearest thumb - that means they are still around the index finger as well as around your thumb (b)!

7.

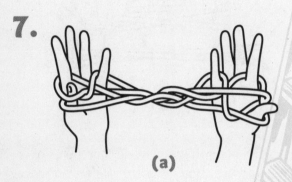 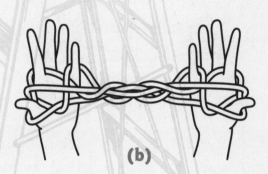

(a)   (b)

There are two loops around each thumb. The 'new' one from the index finger loop is on top, so pull the bottom loop up and over this top loop and take it off the thumb (a) - there's one loop left! Spread your fingers and hands apart and look for a triangle at the base of each hand (b) - check the diagram!

8.

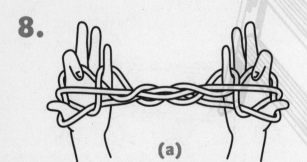 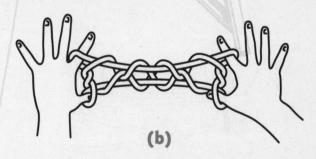

(a)   (b)

Don't drop any loops now - it's the crucial stage! (A hint - keep your hands spread wide, so the strings are fairly taut, even while you work.) Poke your index fingers straight down into these triangles you observed in the previous step (a).

Now as you turn your palms away from you, drop the loops from your little fingers. Spread your fingers apart, wiggling the cord if you need to, and you can see Jacob's Ladder has appeared (b)! Well done if you did this the first time you tried - hardly anybody in the world gets it just right the first time they try this one!

CLIMBING MAN

So if you enjoyed the complexities of Jacob's Ladder, let's continue with the fun, with... The Climbing Man or Man Climbing a Tree - which is thought to have originated in North Queensland, Australia.

1. Begin by creating the index finger base (see page 7).

2.

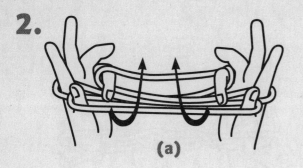

(a)

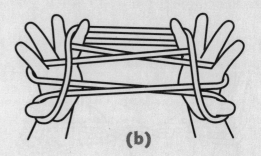

(b)

For your next move reach your little fingers over to the nearest string to you, hook it and then pull it back (a). Now release the original back string (the one which was hooked over both your little fingers originally) - you could use your teeth if that helps (b).

3.

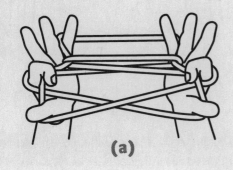

(a)

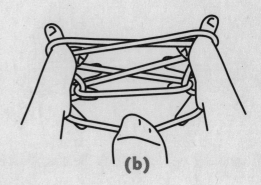

(b)

Now bend your index fingers down and get them to tightly hold the string which goes across them both (a). The next move can be a bit tricky - so be careful! Twist your hands away from you (thumbs on top). With you foot, hold down the far bottom string on the floor (b).

4.

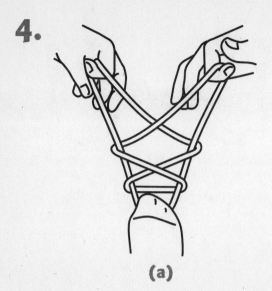

(a)

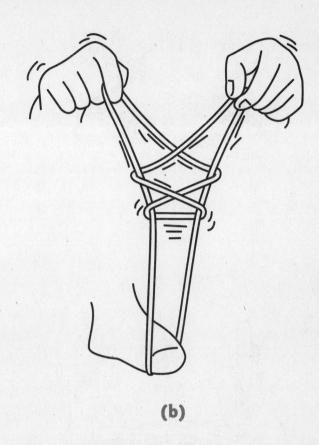

(b)

Holding firmly on to your index fingers strings (and making sure your foot is coping with the bottom string), release all the other strings (a). Now you can dazzle a friend or your family by alternately pulling upwards on each of the index finger strings in turn and make the man climb up his tree (b), or whatever it is he is climbing!

CATCH THE EEL

It is believed this string game comes from Papua New Guinea, and although you create this pattern yourself, the fun really comes when you get a friend to help you at the end - they are in for an amazing surprise!

1.

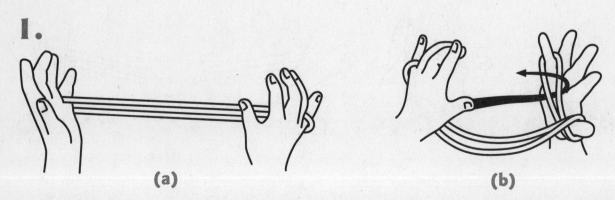

(a)   (b)

Loop your cord over your little fingers. Scoop both strings around your right thumb first of all (a). Now use your left thumb to hook up the strings from your right palm and pull the strings tight (b).

2.

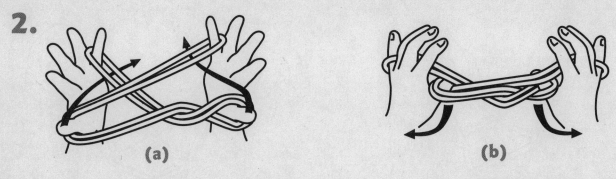

(a) (b)

Use your thumbs to scoop up both the little finger strings (a) and pull them back towards you (b).

3.

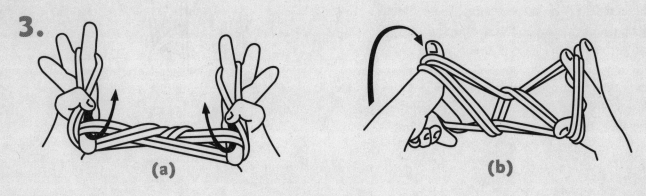

(a) (b)

With your index fingers scoop up the far thumb strings (a). Turn your left hand away from your body - this makes a zig-zag appear in the middle of the strings. You've found the eel (b).

4.

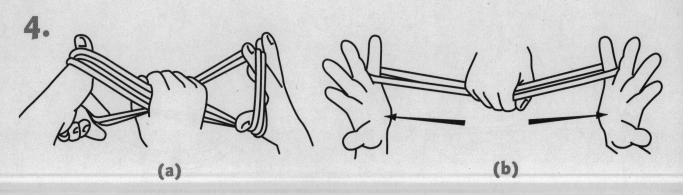

(a) (b)

Now for the fun! Ask a friend to catch or hold the eel. As they do this, release all the strings except your little finger strings, while pulling your hands apart (a). This is the surprise - your action has made the eel disappear from your friend's hand (b)!